CONSTELLATIONS
INTRODUCTION TO THE NIGHT SKY
Science & Technology
Teaching Edition

SPEEDY
PUBLISHING

Speedy Publishing LLC
40 E. Main St. #1156
Newark, DE 19711
www.speedypublishing.com

Constellations have been
an important part of
human society and folklore
since we humans lived
in caves, and, probably,
even before then.

A constellation
is a group of
stars that, when
seen from
Earth, form
a pattern.

The pattern
they form may
take the shape
of an animal,
a mythological
creature, a
man, a woman,
or an inanimate
object.

The origin
of the word
constellation
seems to come
from the Late
Latin term
cōnstellātiō can
be translated
as set of stars.

There are
88 officially
recognized
constellations,
covering the
entire sky.

48 ancient
constellations
listed by
the Greek
astronomer
Ptolemy as
well as 40 new
constellations.

Not all of the constellations are visible from any one point on Earth.

Orion is one of the most visible constellations. Orion is named after a hunter from Greek mythology. Its brightest stars are Betelgeuse and Rigel.

Ursa Major
is visible in
the northern
celestial
hemisphere. It
means "Larger
Bear" in Latin.

Ursa Minor
means "Smaller
Bear" in Latin.
Ursa Minor has
traditionally
been important
for navigation,
particularly by
mariners, due
to Polaris being
the North Star.

Draco is visible
in the far
northern sky.
Draco can be
seen all year
from northern
latitudes.

Aquarius is a
constellation
of the zodiac.
Aquarius is one
of the oldest of
the recognized
constellations
along the
zodiac.

Ophiuchus
is a large
constellation
located around
the celestial
equator.

The Pegasus constellation is named after the flying horse by the same name from Greek mythology.

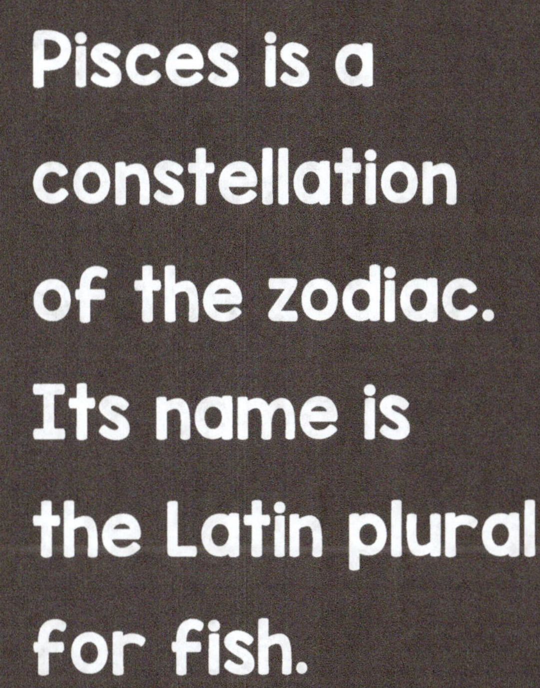

Pisces is a
constellation
of the zodiac.
Its name is
the Latin plural
for fish.

Sagittarius, the "archer," represents the largest constellation in the Southern Hemisphere.

Scorpius
is a large
constellation
located in
the southern
hemisphere
near the
center of the
Milky Way.

Taurus is a large and prominent constellation in the northern hemisphere's winter sky. It is one of the oldest constellations.

Constellations are useful because they can help people to recognize stars in the sky.

Visit
BABY PROFESSOR
EDUCATION KIDS
www.BabyProfessorBooks.com
to download Free Baby Professor eBooks
and view our catalog of new and exciting
Children's Books

www.ingramcontent.com/pod-product-compliance
Lightning Source LLC
Chambersburg PA
CBHW060619120726
48002CB00010B/3031